FROM G9 TO GLOBAL: MY JOURNEY WITH ANURAG

THE LAUGHTER, THE LESSONS, AND THE LEGACY

AKSHI GEHLOT

Made with ♥ on the Notion Press Platform
www.notionpress.com

This book is dedicated to Vodka

(Mmmmmmmmmmmmmmmmm)

oh, and to Nautanki

(Who only drinks LIIT and Redbull)

A massive shoutout to Anirudh, who's always had my back, and to my mom and dad, the real MVPs. Your endless support, spot-on suggestions, and constant love.

Let's keep the vibes rolling as the next chapter unfolds!

Contents

Foreword

Fresh as a daisy!

Preface

Hey Anurag,

By now, you probably know more about me than I've ever shared—seriously, you're in on all the secrets, even the ones I didn't mean to spill! So, when the idea of writing a book started swirling in my head, it only made sense to start with you.

From the start, I've watched others doing great gestures and incredible things for Anurag but, I wanted to create something different, something that truly captures our journey, and out of the box, So here it is—a memory book that's more than just pages; it's a time capsule of every laugh, tear, and wild adventure we've shared.

"From laughs that echoed through the night,
To tears, we've shed in the softest light,
Every page a story, every line a trace,
Of the bond we share, time can't erase.
This isn't just a book—it's our rhyme,
A tribute to our journey, to moments in time,
I hope these words capture our tale so true,
Because with you, Anurag, every chapter feels brand new.
So here's to our past, and what's still in store,
With you, there's always room for more,
In this book of memories, written with love,
Let's cherish each page, with the stars above."

Acknowledgements

To Anurag, my inspiration for this book—you've been the heart of this journey. Thank you for all the memories, the endless laughs, and the shared tears that fill these pages.

To my incredible parents, whose love and wisdom guided me every step of the way—this wouldn't have been possible without you.

And to my fiance, who's always been there with unwavering support, your encouragement kept me going.

This book is a tribute to the moments we've shared and the memories we'll continue to make. Thank you all for being a part of this story.

Prologue

Arre Anurag,

Toh suno, yeh book ekdum filmy style mein likhi hai. Main chahati thi ki humare saare moments, har ek epic adventure, aur woh sab yaadein jo humne milke banayi, woh sab ek jagah pe ho. Jaise ki ek blockbuster movie ke scenes, yeh book bhi humare doston aur family ke saath ke har rangin pal ko capture karti hai.

From the day I walked into G9 as a student, unsure of what I was diving into, to becoming part of your amazing family, it's been one hell of a ride.

I've watched everyone doing enormous things and activities and honestly, I was like, "Hold up, let's do something way cooler." This book isn't just a bunch of pages; it's a full-on treasure trove of our shared laughs, the times we've cried together, and the countless adventures that make our story uniquely ours.

We've been through it all—study sessions that turned into late-night hilarity, epic parties, and those deep, heartfelt conversations. This isn't just about remembering the good times; it's about celebrating every bit of our journey, from the small victories to the big wins.

So, buckle up as you flip through these pages. Each chapter is like a snapshot of our shared life—full of comedy, chaos, and, most importantly, the memories that make life unforgettable. Here's to us, to every moment we've savoured, and to all the crazy, wonderful times still to come.

Chalo, zindagi ka next blockbuster chapter shuru karte hain, ek page ek dhamaka!

CHAPTER ONE

INTRODUCTION

In a world where dreams danced like shadows, obscured by the mist of doubt, I stood on the brink of destiny's door, my heart a compass pointing towards the unknown. My journey had begun, but the path was shrouded in riddles and poetic uncertainties, leading me to a figure whose presence was both puzzling and profound.

"In the labyrinth of dreams, where paths intertwine,
Who guides you through storms, though never benign?
With wisdom wrapped in riddles, and a heart of gold,
Who is this mentor, whose story unfolds?"

Answer: Anurag

Anurag, the man who emerged from the fog like a lighthouse through the tempest, was not just a mentor but an enigma wrapped in a poetic puzzle. His guidance was both cryptic and comforting, a puzzle that invited me to decode the mysteries of my aspirations.

"In the twilight of hope, where the stars align,
Walks a mentor with a purpose, a spirit so divine.
With each step he guides, through the shadows and light,
His wisdom like a beacon, piercing the night."

Anurag was a blend of contrasts—stern yet kind, enigmatic yet clear. He approached life with the flair of a poetic hero, his every word and gesture a verse in the epic of mentorship. To me, he was both the puzzle and the solution, the enigma that stirred my quest for success.

> *"Raaz ki baatein, uski aankhon mein chhupi,*
> *Har paheli ka hal, unki baaton mein mili.*
> *Sath chale hum, is safar mein naye,*
> *Anurag ki baat, jaise chaandni raatein."*

In the dance of our interactions, each argument and resolution was a stanza in our shared poem. Our conflicts, like verses in a ghazal, were laced with passion and learning, revealing deeper truths about ourselves and our bond.

Anurag's presence was like the proverbial "silver lining in the dark cloud." His advice, though sometimes wrapped in riddles, was always a "beacon of hope" guiding me through the fog of uncertainty. He embodied the idiom "when the going gets tough, the tough get going," showing me that true strength lies in persistence.

> *"Every question you ask, every challenge you face,*
> *Is a step towards the future, a part of the race.*
> *With Anurag as the guide, through the highs and the lows,*
> *The journey is a tapestry, where every thread grows."*

As we embark on this journey together, let the riddles and poems be a testament to the twists and turns that define our path. Anurag's guidance is both a mystery and a melody, a dance between the known and the unknown, shaping the story that unfolds with each step we take.

Welcome to the beginning of our tale—a narrative woven with riddles, poems, and the magic of mentorship. Here, every challenge is a verse, every triumph a chorus, and the journey is a saga of dreams and determination.

CHAPTER TWO

JODHPUR MASALA TO LONDON DHAMAKA

"The only way to do great work is to love what you do."
— Steve Jobs

In the vibrant tapestry of Jodhpur, two lives were weaving their own stories in parallel, each a thread in the city's rich fabric, yet utterly disconnected. Imagine us as stars, each blazing in our own orbit, entirely unaware of the other's brilliance. The irony? We were both steeped in the same city's essence, with shared passions and even similar tastes in food, yet our paths never crossed. It's almost as if destiny was keeping us on separate tracks, saving the best plot twist for later. I was the quintessential schoolgirl, the class clown who could turn any mundane lesson into a laugh riot. Known for my cheeky antics and my knack for getting into harmless trouble, I was the girl who brought a sprinkle of mischief to everyone's day. And who would have guessed that this naughty kid, always trying to charm her way through school, would eventually meet someone like Anurag—a mentor who seemed to have stepped straight out of a grand Bollywood saga? Anurag's story, in contrast, was of a different calibre altogether. A prodigy in mathematics with dreams soaring higher than the stars, he was juggling a family business of dry fruits while harbouring ambitions of studying abroad. Despite his talents and aspirations, his family wasn't exactly cheering him on to chase those dreams. Yet, Anurag, with his unyielding determination and resilience, broke through the barriers. Picture him navigating a labyrinth of obstacles, and finally, with a mix of grit and luck, he secured a spot at Greenwich University in London—a milestone many G9 students would later aspire to reach. Back in Jodhpur, I was blissfully unaware of the incredible journey unfolding across the globe. To me, studying abroad seemed like a distant dream, something reserved for the pages of fairy tales. The year was around 2008-2009, and while Anurag was grappling with the real world of London's hustle and bustle, I was just a teenager, juggling school projects and teenage drama. Life in London was a rollercoaster for Anurag. He was immersed in the grind of university life, working multiple part-time jobs to make ends meet, and dealing with the high cost of living. Yet, he managed to keep his spirits high, indulging in London's nightlife, making lifelong friends, and embracing experiences that many only dream of. From the stark contrast of the city's rainy weather to the rich academic environment of Greenwich University, he was living a tale of contrasts—struggling to maintain a balance while savoring every new experience that came his way.

Meanwhile, I was navigating the transition from schoolgirl to a teenager, oblivious to the complexities of Anurag's life in London. My world was confined to the familiar streets of Jodhpur and the everyday joys and challenges of growing up. I didn't grasp the significance of studying abroad or the hardships involved—it was just an idea floating in the background of my youthful dreams. When Anurag returned to India, the fairy tale took an unexpected turn. His homecoming wasn't the glamorous return of a global hero but rather a reality check. He stepped back into Jodhpur and took over his family's dry fruits business—an endeavour he had little passion for, especially after experiencing a different life in the UK. It was a tough adjustment, trading London's vibrant nightlife and international friendships for the quieter pace of Jodhpur's family business. Then came the twist in the tale. Anurag, who had once lived a life of excitement and new experiences, settled into a more traditional role, marrying Swati in a loving arranged marriage. His life, though now more rooted, still had a spark of his previous adventures. With his two best friends—G and P, who remains as elusive as secret agents in our story—he embarked on a new venture. Enter G9. What started as a dream in Anurag's mind, fueled by his own experiences and the desire to help others achieve what he had, soon became a reality. Despite the struggles and challenges of setting up an education consultancy, G9 transformed into a beacon for students aspiring to study abroad. It wasn't just a consultancy; it was a home for countless students, a place where their dreams were nurtured, and their journeys began.

So here we are, on the cusp of a new chapter in our intertwined stories. From separate lives in Jodhpur to the shared experiences at G9, our paths, once so distinct, have converged most unexpectedly and beautifully. But let's linger a little longer on Anurag's story—his journey is the very backbone of this narrative, a tale that has all the elements of a grand epic. Anurag's life was never a straight path; it was a labyrinth filled with twists and turns, highs and lows, yet every step he took was marked by an unwavering determination. As a young man in Jodhpur, Anurag was always more than just a prodigy in mathematics. He was a dreamer, someone whose aspirations reached far beyond the arid landscapes of Rajasthan. His heart was set on a future that wasn't confined to the family business of dry fruits—a venture that, though successful, never quite matched the ambitions that burned within him. When the opportunity to study abroad finally materialized, it wasn't just a personal victory for Anurag; it was a testament to his resilience, a victory against the odds. The journey to Greenwich University wasn't just a flight to a different country—it was a leap into a world filled with possibilities, a world where Anurag could finally start sculpting the life he had always envisioned. The streets of London, with their endless hustle and bustle, became the backdrop for Anurag's transformation. It wasn't an easy journey—juggling studies, part-time jobs, and the ever-looming pressure of financial constraints was no small feat. But London, with its rainy skies and vibrant nights, offered Anurag something that Jodhpur couldn't: the freedom to explore, to fail, and to rise again. In London, Anurag was not just a student; he was an adventurer, navigating the maze of university life while soaking in the rich cultural tapestry that the city had to offer. From late-night study sessions to spontaneous escapades with newfound friends, every experience in London added another layer to the person Anurag was becoming. He wasn't just learning from textbooks; he was absorbing life, understanding what it meant to chase a dream, and what it took to make it a reality.

Yet, life has a way of pulling us back, of reminding us of our roots even when we're soaring high above the clouds. When Anurag returned to Jodhpur, it was with a heart full of memories but also with the realization that life had brought him back to where it all began. The contrast was stark—the vibrant chaos of London was replaced by the quiet rhythm of Jodhpur, and the challenges of university life were swapped for the responsibilities of the family business. Anurag, who had tasted the thrill of independence, now found himself grappling with the expectations of tradition. But if there's one thing that Anurag's journey teaches us, it's that dreams don't die—they evolve. And so did Anurag's. The spark that London had ignited in him didn't fade; instead, it fueled a new vision. G9 was born not just out of a desire to create something new, but out of a passion to help others realize their dreams, just as Anurag had realized his. With his two closest friends, G and P, by his side, Anurag embarked on this new adventure. Together, they built G9 not just as a consultancy, but as a sanctuary for dreamers—a place where aspirations were nurtured, and futures were forged. Anurag's life, though rooted now in Jodhpur, still carries the echoes of London—the lessons learned, the struggles overcome, and the relentless pursuit of a dream. His journey is far from over, and as you turn the pages of this book, you'll see that Anurag's story isn't just about the past; it's a beacon for the future, a reminder that no matter where we start, our dreams can take us places we never imagined.

So, here's to Anurag—the mentor, the dreamer, the doer. His journey is a testament to the power of perseverance, the magic of destiny, and the beauty of chasing a dream, no matter how impossible it may seem. As we step into this new chapter, let Anurag's story inspire us to dream big, to keep going when the road gets tough, and to always believe that the best is yet to come. And now, let's delve deeper into the London that shaped Anurag, the London that became both his battleground and his sanctuary. The city, with its sprawling streets and historic architecture, was a world away from the dusty lanes of Jodhpur. London was not just a city; it was a universe of its own—a place where cultures collided, ideas flourished, and every corner had a story to tell. The Thames River, winding through the heart of the city, witnessed Anurag's countless walks as he contemplated his future, the bridges connecting not just the shores but the phases of his life. Greenwich, the borough that Anurag called home during his university days, was more than just a location—it was a pivotal chapter in his journey. Nestled on the banks of the Thames, Greenwich was steeped in history, from the grandeur of the Royal Observatory to the serene beauty of Greenwich Park. For Anurag, it was a place where the past met the future, where the echoes of maritime history mingled with the buzz of student life. The Greenwich University campus, with its stately buildings and lush green spaces, became Anurag's academic haven. It was here that he honed his skills, diving deep into the world of mathematics while forging friendships that would last a lifetime.

But Greenwich was not just about studies; it was about life in all its vibrant colors. The bustling markets, the quaint cafes, and the lively pubs became Anurag's playground. Weekends were spent exploring the local haunts, whether it was catching a film at the historic Greenwich Picturehouse or grabbing a bite at one of the many food stalls at the Greenwich Market. The nights often extended into the early hours, with Anurag and his friends frequenting the student bars and clubs that dotted the area, each night a new adventure. Student life in London was a whirlwind of experiences—a constant balancing act between the demands of academia and the allure of the city's nightlife. The cost of living was a harsh reality, and Anurag, like many international students, took on multiple part-time jobs to make ends meet. He worked tirelessly, juggling shifts at cafes, tutoring sessions, and any other opportunities that came his way. It was exhausting, but it was also empowering—every pound earned was a step closer to independence, a badge of resilience. Yet, even in the midst of this hustle, Anurag found moments of joy. The friendships he made were not just bonds; they were lifelines, connections that provided support and shared experiences. Together, they navigated the challenges of student life, from late-night study sessions fueled by endless cups of coffee to spontaneous trips around the city, discovering hidden gems and soaking in the culture. London was a city of endless possibilities, and Anurag embraced it all—the good, the bad, and everything in between. Greenwich, with its unique blend of history and modernity, was the backdrop to Anurag's transformation. It was here that he learned the value of hard work, the importance of friendship, and the thrill of exploring the unknown. London, with all its chaos and charm, became a part of Anurag's soul—a place that shaped him, challenged him, and ultimately, prepared him for the journey that lay ahead.

As Anurag's story unfolded in the vibrant streets of London, he was no longer just a student; he was a survivor, a dreamer who had tasted both the bitter and the sweet, and emerged stronger, ready to take on whatever life had in store. The lessons learned in the classrooms of Greenwich and the streets of London were not just academic—they were life lessons, the kind that would guide Anurag long after he had left the city behind. And so, as we turn the page on this chapter of Anurag's life, we carry with us the essence of London—a city that doesn't just shape its inhabitants but leaves an indelible mark on their hearts. For Anurag, London was more than just a place; it was a crucible, a forge where his dreams were tempered and his resolve was steeled. And in the end, it was London that set the stage for the next chapter of his extraordinary journey.

"Us shehar ke rangon mein rang gaye hum,
Anurag ke sapnon mein kho gaye hum,
London ke galiyon ka tha woh ik safar,
Jahan dosti, mehnat, aur khwab sab tha asar.
Mathematics ka tha woh aashiq, sapne uske aasman se
bhi oonche,
Parivaar ka saath na mila, phir bhi jhuke nahi uske kandhe,
Greenwich ki galiyon mein dhoonda apna raasta,
Har pal mein chhupi thi ek nayi dastaan, ek naya qissa.
Jodhpur se nikle the ek sapna lekar,
London ne sikhaya usse jeet ka asli maza chakhkar,
Dosto ke sang guzri woh raatein,
Aur din bhar ki mehnat thi bas apne aap ko paane.
Phir vapas laut aaye apne sheher,
Jahan tha parivaar ka bandhan, aur sapnon ka ek peher,
G9 ka tha woh junoon, ek aangan jahaan sapne sajaaye,
Yeh kahani hai Anurag ki, jo apni raahon pe chala akele,
lekin sabko apne saath laaye.
Ab yeh safar hai kahin rukne ka nahi,
Dhoondte hain naye manzilein, naye raastein har kahin,
Anurag ka junoon hai uss aasman ki oonchaayi,
Jahan khatam hoti hai duniya, uss paar uski kahani hai
likhayi."

"Jodhpur se London, phir wapas apne ghar ki dehleez pe,
Anurag ki yeh kahani hai, jo har dil mein basi ek pyaari se
jagah pe."

Dreams are limitless, and with unshakable determination, resilience, and the right mentorship, even the most daunting obstacles can be transformed into stepping stones. Anurag's journey teaches us that life's twists and turns are not setbacks but opportunities to grow stronger and wiser. His story is a testament to the power of pursuing one's passion, no matter the odds, and the importance of staying true to oneself. Success isn't just about reaching the destination—it's about embracing the journey, cherishing the relationships forged along the way, and turning challenges into triumphs. Ultimately, it's the blend of ambition, perseverance, and the courage to dream big that defines a truly fulfilling life.

CHAPTER THREE

FROM DESKS TO DESTINIES

"Kabhi kabhi kuch paane ke liye kuch khona padta hai, aur kabhi kabhi kuch haar kar hi jeetne wale ko baazigar kehte hain."
— Baazigar

Life was cruising along, and while Anurag was settling into his new role as the go-to guy for dreams of studying abroad, I was knee-deep in the whirlwind of teenage life. It was the usual drama—classroom crushes, late-night gossip sessions with friends, and the eternal struggle of balancing grades with the chaos of adolescence. We still hadn't crossed paths, and our worlds, though destined to collide, were spinning separately.

As the saying goes,

"The best-laid plans of mice and men often go awry."

I was gearing up to finish 11th grade, dreaming of leaving Jodhpur behind to chase my own version of a global adventure. The fever of studying abroad had taken hold of me, and like every teenager with a head full of dreams, I started planning—though, as life would have it, not everything went according to script.

Picture this: I'm fresh out of 12th grade, eyes set on the horizon, ready to conquer the world—or at least get out of Jodhpur. But life, with its quirky sense of humour, threw me a curveball. Plans started to unravel, but instead of wallowing, I told myself, **"Zindagi mein jo bhi hota hai, ache ke liye hota hai."** *Maybe there was something bigger, something better waiting just around the corner. So, finally I did my graduation from India.*

And then, amid this youthful chaos, something unexpected happened. I landed a job in a newbie office in Jodhpur—a temporary detour on my way to what I thought was my true calling. I was neck-deep in work, learning the ropes of corporate life. You know how it goes—early mornings, late nights, and coffee breaks that somehow turned into mini sessions. I didn't realize that amidst the hustle and grind, fate had something else in store for me. The dramatic twist! My fiancé, the ever-reliable guide in my life, casually suggested I check out this place called G9 Abroad Education Consultancy. I'd never heard of it, but hey, if he recommended it, it couldn't be all that bad, right? Still, I was too caught up in my corporate life to pay much attention. But then the day came—the day that would change everything.

"Pehli nazar ka asar, yeh toh hona hi tha."

I finally decided to give G9 a shot. I Googled the number, dialled it with the same casual attitude I had towards life at that point, and the phone rang.

Telephonic Conversation:

Akshi: Hello! Anurag sir? I'm Akshi, and I'm planning to do my master's from abroad.

Anurag (with a teasing edge): Ah, Akshi! We've had quite a few students from your school—sounds like everyone's catching the G9 fever.

Akshi (intrigued): Oh, really? I didn't realize it was such a big thing!

Anurag: Oh, it is. Why don't you come by the office? Let's talk face-to-face—where the real magic happens. Trust me, this could be the beginning of something big.

And just like that, what started as a random suggestion from my fiancé turned into something much more. I still remember that crisp November morning in 2022 when I first walked into the G9 office. Let me set the scene: it was a three-story building, and G9 was perched on the second floor, like a hidden treasure waiting to be discovered. As soon as I stepped inside, it felt like I had entered a different world. The walls were painted in the iconic blue of our Blue City, Jodhpur, and the atmosphere buzzed with the energy of dreams in the making.

> "*Daayen taraf ek audio room tha khaas,*
> *Sapnon ka portal, jahaan sab kuch tha aas-paas.*
> *Reception laal, G9 ki pehchaan,*
> *Beech mein likha, jaise dil ka armaan.*
> *Diwaaron pe tasveerein, visa haath mein sambhaale,*
> *Har chehra muskurahat mein, apne sapne paale.*
> *Yaadon ki kitaab thi, har pal ko sanjoye,*
> *Har tasveer mein jeet ki katha, dil ko chhu jaaye.*
> *Sapne yahan sajte the, umeedon ke rang,*
> *Har musafir ki kahani thi, chhupi har ang.*
> *Dil ke kone mein, ek khaas jagah bani,*
> *G9 ke is safar mein, sabne apni manzil chuni.*"

As I walked out of that first meeting with Anurag, there was a buzz in the air, a feeling that something big was on the horizon. The office wasn't just a place to discuss paperwork and processes—it was where dreams were crafted, shaped, and set on the path to reality. Anurag had a way of making even the most daunting steps seem achievable, and his confidence was contagious. I could feel the weight of his experience, his understanding of every hurdle that lay ahead, and most importantly, his unwavering belief that I would overcome them all. The discussions weren't just about universities and applications; they were about possibilities, about opening doors that I never knew existed. Anurag's guidance was more than just professional—it was deeply personal. He listened to my aspirations, my fears, and my hopes, and in return, he offered not just advice but a roadmap that felt tailor-made for me. As I navigated the next steps, from choosing the right course to preparing for interviews, the connection with Anurag grew stronger. He wasn't just a mentor; he became a friend, a confidant, someone who was genuinely invested in my success. There were moments of doubt, of course—times when the process felt overwhelming, when the road ahead seemed too long and too uncertain. But in those moments, Anurag was there, not just with solutions but with a sense of calm and reassurance that everything would fall into place.

The more I delved into the process, the more I realized that this was about so much more than just getting into a university abroad. It was about discovering my own potential, pushing my limits, and stepping into a new phase of life with confidence. The late-night conversations, the detailed planning sessions, and the constant encouragement from Anurag all became part of a journey that was as enriching as it was challenging. And as each day passed, that initial spark I felt during my first meeting at G9 only grew stronger. There was an undeniable chemistry in the way we both approached this journey—a shared understanding that this wasn't just another application, but the beginning of something transformative. It wasn't just about what lay ahead in a new country, but about the profound change that was already happening within me. The more I worked with Anurag, the more I realized that G9 wasn't just an education consultancy. It was a place where lives were transformed, where every student's story was a testament to resilience, perseverance, and the pursuit of dreams. And as my own journey continued, I knew that this was where my life was truly beginning, not just in a new country, but in a new chapter that would define my future. Every meeting, every conversation, every decision felt like a step towards something greater—a future filled with promise, excitement, and endless possibilities.

The story of my journey was no longer just mine; it was intertwined with Anurag's, with G9's, with the countless students who had walked through those same doors and emerged stronger, wiser, and ready to take on the world. This was more than just a process; it was the beginning of a lifelong adventure, one that I would carry with me wherever I went. And in that realization, I found not just hope but a deep sense of purpose—a clarity that this journey was exactly where I was meant to be, guided by the hand of fate and the unwavering support of a mentor who had become family.

> "*In Jodhpur's lanes, where dreams were spun,*
> *I danced through days and teenage fun.*
> *With classroom crushes and gossip shared,*
> *A world so small, yet dreams declared.*
> *Anurag's journey far and wide,*
> *In London's streets, he did reside.*
> *With math and dreams, a star so bright,*
> *He faced his struggles, took his flight.*
> *While I was lost in teenage flair,*
> *Dreams of abroad danced in the air.*
> *Plans were laid, but life would jest,*
> *Unraveling paths, I took the test.*
> *From Jodhpur's job to G9's door,*
> *A twist of fate, a chance to explore.*
> *The office buzzed with hopes anew,*
> *A world of dreams, both old and new.*
> *Anurag's voice, a guiding light,*
> *In a world that felt so right.*
> *He listened close, with wisdom deep,*
> *In every challenge, took a leap.*
> *Our meeting sparked a flame so bright,*
> *A shared excitement, pure delight.*
> *Not just a plan, but a journey grand,*
> *With Anurag's help, I'd take my stand.*
> *Late nights and dreams, the road we paved,*
> *In G9's halls, my path was saved.*
> *Not just a visa, but a life renewed,*

With every step, my dreams pursued.
Through every meeting, every plan,
My journey changed, as fate began.
G9 was more than just a place,
It was a beacon, a warm embrace.
A future bright, with promise clear,
In every challenge, I found cheer.
With Anurag's guide, I'd boldly go,
To chase my dreams, let the world know.
In every story, every line,
A tale of hope, of dreams divine.
A journey shared, a life reborn,
In every sunrise, a new dawn. "

In the vibrant city of Jodhpur, two seemingly unrelated lives were unfolding—Anurag, a prodigy in mathematics, was navigating the bustling streets of London, while I was caught up in the whirlwind of teenage life. Anurag's journey was a testament to perseverance; he tackled rigorous academic challenges at Greenwich University while juggling multiple part-time jobs to make ends meet. Despite the stark contrast between London's rainy weather and Jodhpur's sunny disposition, Anurag embraced every obstacle with unyielding determination, forging lifelong friendships and soaking up every experience the city had to offer. Meanwhile, my life was a blend of school dramas and adolescent dreams. The concept of studying abroad was a distant fantasy, something that felt like it belonged to the pages of fairy tales. As I neared the end of 12th grade, I was eager to escape Jodhpur and explore new horizons, but life had its own plans. Instead of setting off on an adventure, I found myself starting a new job in Jodhpur, grappling with the realities of corporate life. It was a routine filled with early mornings, late nights, and the occasional coffee break, with the dream of studying abroad lingering at the back of my mind. Everything changed when my fiancé suggested I check out G9 Abroad Education Consultancy. The name was unfamiliar, but his recommendation was enough for me to give it a shot. On a crisp November morning in 2022, I walked into the G9 office. The three-story building, painted in Jodhpur's signature blue, was a beacon of hope and opportunity. Inside, the atmosphere buzzed with the energy of dreams being realized. And there was Anurag, now a mentor at G9, whose journey from London to Jodhpur had brought him back to help others achieve their aspirations. Our meeting was more than just a consultation; it was the beginning of a transformative journey. Anurag's insights into the study abroad process, combined with his own experiences in London, made the seemingly daunting process feel manageable and achievable. His support and belief in my potential provided the encouragement I needed to navigate the complexities of applications and preparations. As I delved deeper into the process with Anurag's guidance, I realized how our paths had unexpectedly converged. From separate lives in Jodhpur to a shared journey at G9, our stories intertwined in a way that was both surprising and meaningful. Anurag's return from London and my transition from a high school student to a working professional were linked by the common thread of pursuing dreams with determination and passion.

"*Alright, listen up! Here's the lowdown: life can be a wild ride with crazy twists. Anurag was grinding hard in London, balancing college, work, and all the ups and downs of city life. Back in Jodhpur, I was just vibing through high school and dreaming about escaping to chase my own goals.*

But then, things got real. Instead of jumping straight into my dream college, I found myself in a new job in Jodhpur—definitely not part of the plan. My fiancé suggested checking out G9 Abroad Education Consultancy, and that turned out to be the ultimate game changer.

So, I walked into G9, and it was like stepping into a whole new world. Anurag, who'd been through the London grind, was now the guide I didn't know I needed. He made the whole study abroad thing feel like a real possibility instead of just a distant dream.

Here's the kicker: every curveball life throws at you is just setting you up for something epic. Anurag's London hustle and my unexpected job detour led us to meet at G9, where things started to click. It's like the universe was working behind the scenes, setting the stage for something amazing.

The moral? Don't sweat the setbacks. They're just life's way of redirecting you to where you're meant to be. Keep grinding, stay positive, and don't be afraid to take those detours. With the right guidance and a whole lot of determination, you can turn your wildest dreams into reality. Embrace the journey, because every twist is just another step towards your ultimate goal."

Finally, the universe aligned, and I found myself face-to-face with Anurag. He wasn't just another consultant; he was the gatekeeper to my future, the mentor who would eventually become like family. We talked about everything—the exams, the prep, the excitement of stepping into a new world. As we said our goodbyes that day, there was a spark, a shared excitement for the journey ahead. **"Yeh jo hum milte hain, aisa lagta hai ke kahin kuch naya hone wala hai."** Our meeting felt like the beginning of something big, and little did I know, it was the start of a chapter that would change my life forever.

CHAPTER FOUR

The Beginning of Something New

"The future belongs to those who believe in the beauty of their dreams."
– Eleanor Roosevelt

So, we finally met. G9 Abroad Education—was it just another consultancy, or did it feel like stepping into a different world? The vibe was electric, the kind that gives you goosebumps, like you're on the brink of something big. You know how in Bollywood movies, the hero walks into the frame, and everything slows down? That's exactly how it felt like the universe was setting the stage for something epic.

"Kehte hain agar kisi cheez ko dil se chaho... toh poori kainaat usse tumse milane ki koshish mein lag jaati hai," right?

After I got home, I was buzzing with excitement, like I'd just unlocked a new level in a game. Joining G9 felt like I'd gained superpowers overnight—there was something about that place, the energy, the people. A week later, in November 2022, I finally joined the class. Managing everything wasn't easy; juggling office work and classes was like walking a tightrope. My office folks were a bunch of buzzkills, except one, always breathing down my neck, never understanding that I had bigger dreams. I had to tell them I was taking graphic design classes—*"corporate wale kya samjhenge yaar, aish karne ka mann toh unka kabhi hota hi nahin," right?* On the first day at G9, I walked in with full swag, like a boss.

High-waist jeans, swag toh full-on,
T-shirt tucked, style mein jaan.
Highlight waale baal, leherate yoon,
Specs on point, jaise heroine ka mood hoon.

I felt like a cool dude, ready to conquer. The vibe in the class was something else—everyone was chilled out but focused. Anurag, my mentor, kicked things off by asking me to speak on the calendar.

Calendar?

Seriously?

I mean, I was a bright student, a university scholar, but somehow, standing there, I froze. What was that? Nerves? A new kind of hesitation? But Anurag made it all so easy with his "chill maar, itna sochne ka nahin" attitude. The first few days were all about settling in, with a bit of attitude and a lot of swag. Every new member wanted to know who this new girl was—classic boys, always curious. Anurag, on the other hand, kept reminding me to bring a notebook. But come on, I'm all about style—who needs a boring notebook when a diary looks so much cooler, right? Managing office and G9 became a bit of a grind. Every morning was a rush—class first, then off to the office, and back to studying. It was a lot, but I didn't give up. After six months, I put in my resignation. *"Mujhe apni life aur bhi advance banani thi, aur yeh office waale kabhi samajhte hi nahin."*My focus was on going abroad, and I wasn't going to let anything hold me back. During this phase, things got hectic. I missed a few classes, and the fun times I was having at G9 seemed to slip away. But once I left my job, I became a regular again, diving into the classes with new energy. Anurag and I didn't talk much during this time; it was just the usual student-teacher dynamic. But G9 had this magic—*jo bhi aata, bas wahin ka ho kar reh jaata,* and I was no exception. As time passed, I made new friends, and for the first time, we all went out together to a café. Anurag, being the party guy he is, planned the outing. It was a chilly winter day, and I showed up in a pink sweatshirt, black jeans, and a high ponytail—felt like a cute Barbie doll. We all sat around, chatting and laughing like we'd known each other for ages. Anurag, ever the host, ordered his usual vodka, while I sipped on a Red Bull. *"Bhai ne apne style mein cheers maara, aur maine bhi saath diya,"* and just like that, it was one of those nights you don't forget.

The next day at G9, the atmosphere was different—everyone had a little extra pep in their step, a little more sparkle in their eye. It was like the café outing had turned us from classmates into a squad. The way we all recapped the night before felt like we were reliving scenes from a Bollywood movie. Every joke, every laugh, it was like a montage of friendship that played on repeat in our minds. Anurag, always the life of the party, had his signature smirk, as if he knew that night was one for the books. But amidst all the laughter, there was a part of me that started to drift. I could feel the weight of everything—studies, expectations, the future—slowly pulling me away from the fun. The casual vibe at G9, the way we all connected, it was still there, but I wasn't. I started skipping classes, thinking I could catch up later. Maybe it was the pressure, or maybe I just needed a break. But in those moments away from G9, I realized something important—this journey wasn't just about flying abroad, it was about everything in between.

When I finally decided to get back on track, I knew I had to get serious. The fun times were great, but they wouldn't get me my visa. Anurag, with his usual chill but firm attitude, suggested I book my IELTS exam. It was like a wake-up call—no more slacking, no more distractions. So I did just that, booked my exam, and returned to G9 with a renewed focus. It wasn't easy, though. The doubts, the fears, they all crept in as the exam date approached. But every time I sat in that classroom, every time I saw Anurag's casual confidence, I felt a little bit stronger. Getting back into the groove of studying was like stepping into a new chapter of my life. The random chats with Anurag became more meaningful, more focused on what really mattered. It wasn't just about acing the exam; it was about understanding that this was just one step in a much larger journey. The fun and the partying had their place, but so did the hard work and the late-night study sessions. And then came the exam day. Walking into that room, I felt like I was walking onto a stage—lights, camera, action! The pressure was on, but so was the excitement. It was like all those months at G9 had led up to this moment. I could hear the voiceover in my head, narrating every step, every thought, just like in a Bollywood movie. The exam was tough, no doubt, but I kept thinking about everything Anurag had said, all the motivation, all the advice. And when it was finally over, I walked out feeling like I had just completed the climax scene of a blockbuster.

But the story didn't end there. Waiting for the results was like that suspenseful moment before the big reveal in a movie. Every day felt like an eternity, but I knew I had done my best. And when the results finally came in—boom! I had passed! It was a moment of pure joy, like when the hero finally wins against all odds. But the real drama was yet to come—the visa application process. June rolled around, and I was ready to apply for my September visa. But as always, my journey took its own sweet time. It was like being stuck in a never-ending suspense thriller, with twists and turns at every corner. But with the blessings of everyone around me, and a special thanks to Anurag's unwavering support, the long-awaited news finally came in July: my visa had been approved. The relief, the excitement, the sense of accomplishment—it all came rushing in like a tidal wave, sweeping away the doubts and fears that had lingered for so long. As I finally prepared to fly to the UK, I couldn't help but reflect on how far I had come—from the girl who walked into G9 with dreams in her eyes to the woman now ready to conquer the world. And throughout it all, Anurag had been there, not just as a mentor, but as a friend, a guide, a constant presence. G9 wasn't just a consultancy; it was a place where dreams took flight, where friendships were forged, and where life lessons were learned. The memories we created, the lessons we learned, and the bonds we formed—they were all a part of this incredible journey. Every laugh, every tear, every moment of doubt, and every moment of triumph—they all made this journey worth it. And as I step onto that plane, ready to start a new chapter in my life, I know that G9, Anurag, and everyone who has been a part of this journey will always hold a special place in my heart.

And so, as I board that flight, I realize that this is just the beginning. The real journey is yet to come, and I'm ready for whatever life throws at me next. Because if there's one thing I've learned from all of this, it's that no matter how many challenges come your way, no matter how many times life tries to knock you down, you have to keep going, keep fighting, and keep believing in yourself. And who knows? Maybe one day, someone will tell my story, just like I've told this one—a story of dreams, determination, and the incredible power of never giving up.

> *"In the halls of G9, where dreams intertwine,*
> *A story began with laughter and wine.*
> *From notes in a diary to secrets shared,*
> *A journey of growth, where no one was spared.*
> *Through challenges faced and lessons learned,*
> *A bond was forged, where passions burned.*
> *Now as the final chapter nears its end,*
> *Tell me, dear reader, where does the story bend?*
> *Is it in the cheers of a night well-spent,*
> *Or in the dreams that were heaven-sent?*
> *The answer lies where the heart does roam,*
> *In the place we call, our second home.*
> *What am I?"*

With a heart full of memories, a mind full of dreams, and a spirit ready to soar, I take my first step into the future. And as the plane takes off, I can't help but smile, knowing that this journey is far from over—it's just getting started.

"*Dil mein sapne, aankhon mein roshni,*
G9 ke galiyon mein, hui kahaani nai.
"Ruk jaana nahin, tu kahin haarke,"
Jeans high-waist mein, sapno se bhare.
"Mere sapno ki rani kab aayegi tu?"
Iss naye safar mein, tera intezaar ho raha hai ab kyun?
Chal mere saath, yeh raaste hain naye,
"Zindagi ek safar hai suhana," hum sapne sajaaye.
"Kabhi kabhie Aditi, zindagi mein yun hi,"
Zindagi ka safar, ab toh hai shuru,
Dil se dil tak, bas khushiyon ka jadoo.
Chill maar ke baatein thi, coffee aur vodka,
"Koi kahe kehta rahe, kitna bhi humko deewana,"
Class mein hustle, aur café ki chaska.
Anurag ne dikhayi, har raste ki raahein,
"Lakshya toh har haal mein paana hai," sapno ko paayein.
"Jeene ke hain chaar din, baaki hain bekaar din,"
Lekin humne toh har pal ko jiya, jaise ho yeh golden din.
Chal mere saath, yeh raaste hain naye,
"Yeh haseen wadiyan," hum sapne sajaaye.
"Chak de! Chak de India," safar ka hai junoon,
Zindagi ka safar, ab toh hai shuru,
Dil se dil tak, bas khushiyon ka jadoo.
Jo thha ek sapna, ab hai haqeeqat,
"Mitwa... kahein dhadkan hai tujhse kya,"
IELTS ka result, aur visa ka paighaam.
July mein mili, khushiyon ki wo dastaan,
"Yeh jo des hai tera," udte hue plane se, yeh dil gaaye gaana.
Hawaon mein udta, manzil ki talash mein,
"Chhaiyyan chhaiyyan," sapne leharayein aasman mein.
"Ek ladki ko dekha toh aisa laga,"
G9 ki galiyon mein, sab kuch alag sa laga.
"Badtameez dil, badtameez dil," jahan tha,
Lekin sapne poore karne ka junoon, hamesha tha.

Chal mere saath, yeh raaste hain naye,
"Kabhi kabhi Aditi, zindagi mein yun hi koi apna lagta hai,"
hum sapne sajaaye.
"Kal ho naa ho," lekin aaj toh jeene de,
Zindagi ka safar, ab toh hai shuru,
Dil se dil tak, bas khushiyon ka jadoo.
Yeh safar abhi hai shuru, dil mein hai jo junoon,
"Ghoomar ghoomar," G9 se chali thi kahaani, ab aasman
hai gunaahoon.
Udti raho, khilte raho, har pal hai naye sapno ka junoon,
"Pal pal dil ke paas, tum rehti ho," yeh safar hai khwaabon
ka,
Jisne diya hai naya junoon.
"

**So, what happens next after the IELTS? Well, "picture
abhi baaki hai mere dost!"**

"JAZBAAT AUR JUNOON"

"Zindagi mein haarna bura nahi hai, lekin haar ke ruk jaana galat hai. Samasyaein aayengi, par inhi samasyaon mein chhupi hai jeet ki kunji." -Jaya Kishore

The thrill of stepping into G9's world left me buzzing with excitement, a place where education felt like an art, not a task. I was confident—no, overconfident—that the IELTS was just another stepping stone. After all, I was a proud alumna of Rajmata Krishna Kumari Girls' Public School, where English was second nature to us. Life has a way of humbling you, reminding you that not everything goes as planned. Anurag, my ever-persistent mentor, kept urging me to aim for a Band 7. ***"Easy peasy,"*** I told myself, while our conversations started to flow more naturally—nothing too deep, just about Jodhpur, people, and the odd joke here and there. Anurag had this uncanny ability to get people to spill their secrets, but I was a tough nut to crack. My style was my shield—hot, classy clothes, strutting into class like it was a runway. G9 wasn't just a learning; it was a vibe, a scene where fashion met education.

The day arrived, and I set off for Ahmedabad, brimming with self-assurance. I still remember the date, February 9th, 2023—my speaking test. I aced it, or so I thought. The first call I made afterwards was to Anurag.

Akshi: "Hey! I just finished my speaking test. It was amazing! I totally nailed it."

Anurag had hope, just like me, that I would score a Band 7. But life, *"Zindagi ka har mod ek seekh hai, bas hume uss seekh ko samajhne ki zaroorat hai."* Every twist and turn in life teaches us something. I spent the rest of the day enjoying Ahmedabad with my family and friends. We roamed the streets, carefree, with the exam still lingering in the back of my mind. The next morning, I called Anurag, who wished me luck before I headed into the exam hall. IELTS, which I had assumed would be easy, was anything but. When I sat down to write, my confidence wavered, and in my head, I could only think, "Jai Mata Di." It was in that moment I realized, "Overconfidence ka phal hamesha kadwa hota hai." The exam was tougher than I had anticipated. I did my best and walked out of the centre, my mind racing with doubts, but I shared the experience with Anurag and my family, who remained optimistic. After a night's stay, we headed back to Jodhpur. I met Anurag and shared more details about the trip and the exam. I was still hopeful, but when the results came in a week later, I was in for a shock—Band 6. It felt like a slap in the face. How could someone so confident, someone who prided herself on her English, score this low? The comparison game began, and it was brutal. Other students, ones I considered less fluent, had scored better, which shattered my confidence. I cried, not just because of the score, but because my self-worth felt like it had taken a hit.

But words rang in my ears: *"Asli safalta wahi hai, jab gir ke hum dobara uthne ki himmat rakhein."* True success is when you dare to rise after a fall. Anurag and my family didn't let me stay down for long. They encouraged me to try again, with more determination and less arrogance. I bought a proper notebook, a decent pen, and started my studies with renewed dedication. The fun and light-hearted moments continued, but there was a newfound seriousness in my approach.

During this time, Anurag and I got to know each other better. I remember visiting Men's Café with my friends, a place where Anurag loved the red pasta. For the first time, I sent him a picture of the place on WhatsApp.

Akshi: "Look where I am! Men's Cavé, your favourite!"

Anurag (with emojis): "Aha! Enjoy! Save some pasta for me ?."

I felt a tinge of shyness but also excitement. Anurag was cool, and our conversations began to flow more naturally. Then, he planned a trip to Bangkok with his family with his two adorable kids, Pahal and Aarav. Before leaving, he asked me to come to class and practice more. But without my mentor around, the motivation to attend was low, and I ended up practising at home instead. I sent him an invitation to Prashadi Hanuman Janamutsav, and he replied in his usual manner, even though he was miles away. When Anurag returned from his trip, I had already slipped into a routine of not attending classes. You know how it is—once you take a break, it's hard to get back. But that's where the real story begins. On April 14th, I received a call from him, not from his number but from his intern.

Anurag: "Hey Akshi! I'm back in town. Why aren't you coming to class?"

Akshi: "Oh, welcome back! How was your trip?"

Anurag: "Amazing! Lots of stories to share. But more importantly, hume exam dena hai, ya yaha sirf baatein banani hain?"

Akshi: "Of course, dena toh hai."

Anurag: "Okay, now you owe me a party"

Akshi: "Let's do it!"

Anurag was shocked. He hadn't expected me to agree so quickly. He might have thought I was joking. He felt shy, and in my head, I could hear a Bollywood track playing, setting the tone for what felt like the start of something new. *"Yeh toh bas shuruaat hai,"* I thought, feeling the excitement of a teenage, with all the drama and suspense.

Anurag's unexpected call from his intern was a jolt of reality that brought me back from my self-imposed hiatus. His return from Bangkok marked a turning point, a reminder that my journey was far from over. The anticipation of reuniting with my mentor filled me with a new sense of purpose. As I reflected on our conversation, I couldn't help but think of how life often unfolds like a screenplay—full of twists and turns.

In those days of waiting and preparing, my thoughts often turned to poetic reflections on the student-teacher relationship:

"Har ek nayi manzil par, ek nayi raah milti hai,
Teacher ki guidance se, raatein bhi roshni se bharein.
Seekhne ka safar kabhi khatam nahi hota,
Har ek challenge mein nayi seekh chhupi hoti hai."

"

Anurag's persistence was a constant reminder of the goals I had set for myself. Our conversations, though focused on exam preparations, carried an undercurrent of motivation and resolve. I could sense the weight of his expectations, and it pushed me to rise above my earlier setbacks. The excitement of reconnecting was tinged with the seriousness of the task at hand:

"Zindagi ki is raahon mein, sab kuch seekhna padta hai,
Teacher ki baaton ko samajhna, aur phir usi ke saath aage badhna padta hai.
Har pal ki mehnat ko pehchaan na,

Aise hi milta hai, success ka asli asar."

As I resumed my preparations with renewed vigor, I felt like I was moving into a new phase of my journey. The playful banter between Anurag and me continued, but it was clear that our focus had shifted to the practical aspects of achieving my goals. Each study session became a testament to the hard work we had both put in:

"Mehnat ki raahon par, kabhi na rukna chahiye,
Teacher ki guidance se, sapne sach karna chahiye.
Har ek lesson ka hissa, ek kadam aur aage badhna,
Yahi hai safalta ki raah, yahi hai sahi dastaan."

Our dynamic evolved, and with each interaction, I felt more attuned to the lessons Anurag imparted. It was not just about passing an exam; it was about embracing the process, understanding the value of perseverance, and reflecting on the journey:

"Har ek mushkil raaste mein, ek naya junoon jagta hai,
Teacher ki baaton mein, nayi raahon ka gyaan milta hai.
Seekhne ki is raah pe, kabhi na rukna hai,
Yahi hai zindagi ka asal maqsad, yahi hai asli safar."

The final stretch before the exam was a period of intense preparation, and with Anurag's encouragement, I found the strength to face my challenges head-on. Our conversations and his unwavering support reminded me that this was not just an academic challenge but a personal journey of growth and self-discovery. As I approached the exam, I knew I had come a long way, and the lessons learned were invaluable:

"Exam ki raahon mein, har pal ka hai mahatva,
Teacher ki mehnat ka, har pal hai naya rang.
Seekh ke is safar ko, pura karna hai humein,
Yahi hai zindagi ka sachcha rang, yahi hai asli sang."

With these thoughts guiding me, I felt prepared to tackle whatever lay ahead. The journey with Anurag and the lessons from G9 were more than just academic—they were the foundation of a new chapter in my life.

"Yeh toh bas shuruaat hai," I thought. Little did we know, that was just the beginning of our story.

OFFICE ME ADVENTURE, OR KAAM KA NAAM?

"Sometimes, the strongest bonds are hidden in plain sight, where the truth is known only to those who dare to see beyond the illusion."

The morning air was thick with anticipation as I walked into the classroom, the chatter of the well spend time still fresh in everyone's mind. Little did they know, not all of G9 had been there—only a few special members, or so they believed. The reality was far more intricate, a secret between Anurag and me.

As I settled in, my mind shifted to the IELTS exam. Anurag was relentless, determined that I would clear it this time. We decided on the computer-based test, believing it would give me an edge. I booked the exam with a mix of excitement and nerves, confident this was it—this was when I'd finally make it. G9 was our playground, and every student had their plans, but ours was different. Anurag and I, both party enthusiasts, had more in mind than just an exam.

> *"May 4ᵗʰ, the date was set,*
> *finally met.*
> *Grey jeans, red tee, nerves on high,*
> *time to fly!*
> *Laughs, slow beats, sunrise glow.*
> *Anurag, my guide, kept me on track,*
> *Quizzing me hard, no confidence lack."*

I quickly prepared for the exam. The test centre was within walking distance, and I nailed my speaking session. Post-exam, I came back to the jodhpur, then we celebrated with a hearty meal—rajma rice and chole bhature—and then it was time to prepare for the night's adventure.

> *"That evening, we transformed into stars of the night,*
> *Dressed to impress, stepping out in style, ready to ignite.*
> *was calling, the vibe electric and wild,*
> *A young, vibrant crowd where we'd blend in, no denial.*
> *Outfits sassy, cool, and hotter than fire,*
> *We hit the dance floor, living our desire.*
> *"Kaali Kaali Zulfon Ke" set the stage,*
> *Our debut song, freeing us from any cage.*
> *The beats dropped, and so did our fears,*
> *We danced like no tomorrow, shedding all tears.*
> *From "Lungi Dance" to "Nashe Si Chadh Gayi,"*
> *Every beat made us soar, every move fly.*
> *"Kala Chashma" had us grooving in sync,*
> *While "London Thumakda" made the night blink.*
> *Lost in the music, we became one with the sound,*
> *A Bollywood dream where only joy was found.*
> *Each song was a chapter, each move a tale,*
> *We were the leads in this filmy trail.*

> *The magic of the night wrapped around us tight,*
> *As we danced through the songs, into the light.* "

Fueled by LIITs and vodka, we danced without care, Who knew if this was the end or just the start,
Of something wild, something from the heart. The night was tight, and so was I, Floating in a haze, under the starry sky. The night blurred, pulses high, nothing could compare. Back in the room, with memories so sweet, We laughed and recapped, not missing a beat. The night might have ended, but the energy stayed,
A night full of magic, where we all played.

As the music faded and the night began to wane, a sudden realization struck me—Anurag's guidance was more than just about exams; it had become a way of life. The party lights dimmed, but the echoes of his advice resonated louder than ever.

In a surprising turn, my mentor had a bold idea: to clear out all distractions so I could focus better. I followed his advice closely, blocking out every notification and message that wasn't crucial. Among those I blocked was someone very special—someone whose presence mattered deeply to me. This person was important, but I made the choice to block them as well, believing it was the right step for my journey.

Can you guess who this special person was?

The next day, the tension of the night before settled into a quiet contemplation. I looked at my phone, the screen devoid of familiar faces, and felt a pang of isolation. Yet, in the midst of this self-imposed solitude, Anurag's support had never felt more tangible. His words had shaped my actions, but now, faced with the emptiness of my blocked contacts, I questioned the price of this obedience.

Anurag called later that afternoon. The conversation was casual, filled with the usual banter and light-hearted advice. But there was an undercurrent of concern in his voice that I hadn't expected.

Anurag: "Hey, Akshi! How's it going? After blocking everyone?

Akshi (hesitantly): "Yeah, I thought it was necessary. You know, to focus better. Even... even **my boyfriend."**

There was a pause, a silence that felt heavy with unspoken words.

Anurag: "I see. Well, you did what you thought was best, but remember, balance is key. It's not just about blocking out distractions but also about keeping the right connections alive."

His words were a subtle reminder of the complexity of trust and guidance. It was a cliffhanger, a moment of introspection where I had to balance my faith in Anurag with the real-world implications of my choices. The suspense of how to navigate this newfound solitude and reconcile with the emotional impact of my actions loomed large.

As I hung up, I was left to ponder: had my devotion to Anurag led me astray, or was this a necessary step in the journey towards self-discovery and focus? The plot thickened, and the resolution remained uncertain, but one thing was clear—this journey was far from over.

The next day was a blend of nerves and preparation. dressed in our finest. The formal dinner that night on a rooftop with stunning views and lively youth was a perfect end to the day. The atmosphere was one of celebration and youth, our group looking so ultra-cool that others wanted to join us. The exam day was a breeze; the paper went well, and we spent the rest of the time discussing questions and laughing about our answers. It was always my job to grab the Zomato orders, and we enjoyed a tasty lunch. As the exam was a success, we decided to party again, a place known for its awesome Bollywood tracks. We danced a night of pure fun and frolic. The dance moves were unforgettable, especially when we flirted with the girl gang group, creating a scene that was nothing short of filmy:

"Sunn zara... jaan-e-jahaan, Aaj humne kasam khayi hai, Hum pyar ke rang mein, yun hi rahoongi."

But like all good things, was filled with nostalgia and emotion as we reminisced about the moments we had shared—the crazy dance moves, the tasty food. Who knew a mentor could become so close, so much a part of my family? I was my usual shy self when it came to eating, which always worried them. The conversations flowed as we had memories, from our studies to the fun we had.

Four days later, the results came in. The suspense was killing me, and I let the public decide what the outcome might have been. But with every discussion, I realized that this journey was far from over.

We booked it, The reasons were ours alone, hidden from the world. what called to us once more, and we answered, this time knowing that it wasn't just about partying—it was about understanding each other, about growing closer. Anurag, in those moments, became more than just a mentor; he became family. I followed his guidance, trusting him implicitly, and hoped he understood how much it all meant to me. The suspense builds again— What happened next? The answers lie in the future, in the choices we make, and in the paths we follow. The journey wasn't over; it was just beginning. We didn't stop, even when the IELTS results didn't match our expectations. Our last attempt was filled with hope, determination, and a deep sense of purpose. It was a journey of learning, of pushing boundaries, of realizing that some things aren't written in the stars, but that doesn't mean you stop reaching for them. Anurag and I studied, we took the exam, and for the first time, we allowed ourselves to be vulnerable, to open up, to truly connect. So did another chapter of this journey. The score remained elusive, a band 6 that just wouldn't shift, but I didn't lose hope. I had learned too much, and grown too much, to let this defeat me. Life has taught me that what you need will come to you, but only if you work for it, only if you refuse to give up. In Uttarakhand, surrounded by family, another result came, and once again, it was the same. But I knew now that the journey was just as important as the destination. I would go to the UK for my master's—of that, I was certain. And as I reflected on everything that had happened, I realized that it was because of Anurag that I had come this far. His mentorship, and his friendship, were the key, and for that, I will always be grateful.

The journey was tough, especially when everyone around you seemed to be achieving their goals while you stood still. But I didn't lose hope. My dream of going to the UK for my master's was still alive, and I knew I would achieve it, thanks to Anurag's unwavering support and guidance. Through all the ups and downs, the fights, and the reunions, Anurag changed me, taught me new things, and made me a stronger person. We fought like crazy, but we always reunited even stronger. Those dinners, drives, and group parties were filled with both love and battles, but they shaped who I am today. And now, as I look back, I know that the IELTS journey was just the beginning. I had to give up on that specific goal, but it didn't mean giving up on my dream. With a scholarship in hand, I was on the path to finding a new way to reach the UK.

As the suspense mounted, the future held its secrets tightly. The journey wasn't ending; it was evolving. Even when the IELTS results fell short of our expectations, we persisted with hope and determination. This final attempt was about more than just results—it was about pushing boundaries and understanding that some goals require more than luck; they require relentless effort.

Interactive Elements:

Puzzle: As you reflect on the journey, solve this puzzle to discover the core of your determination.

1. Unscramble the letters to reveal the key theme of our journey:

- **DCTREAIION**
- **NSIEAYV**

Complete the following sentence to uncover the significance of persistence in our journey:

-

"Success is not just about ______________, but about the journey and the effort."

Decision Point: Choose your path:

- **Path A: If you choose to focus on the journey and the experiences along the way, you will emphasize learning and growth.**
- **Path B: If you choose to focus solely on the destination and final results, you will concentrate on achieving the set goals.**

By interacting with these elements, you can better understand the essence of our journey. The final score remained a Band 6, but the true lesson was in the perseverance and growth we experienced. Surrounded by family in Uttarakhand, another result came through, and once again, it was a Band 6. But this time, I understood that the journey was as important as the destination. With a scholarship in hand, I was ready to find a new path to reach the UK.

Reflecting on everything, I realized that Anurag's mentorship and friendship were pivotal. He had transformed me, teaching me resilience and strength through our highs and lows. Despite the challenges, the fights, and the reunions, the IELTS journey was merely the beginning. I had to adapt my plans, but I never gave up on my dream. With renewed determination and Anurag's unwavering support, I was set on the path to achieving my goal in a new way.

And so, the suspense continues—what happens next? How will I achieve my goal? The answers are out there, waiting to be discovered, and I'm ready to find them.

> *"G9 ke boss hai Anurag, full-on swag,*
> *Chhoti si pony, lekin attitude ka tag.*
> *"Arre kya hai, yaar? Sharat haar jayega,"*

Woh jokes mein bhi gyaan ka tadka lagayenge.
"Pagal hai kya?" unki aam dialogue hai,
Har baat mein ek twist, jise sunna sabko maza aata hai.
Chhoti si pony, lekin style mein zabardast,
Har challenge ko leke, woh hai full-on mast.
"Chal, party dede!" woh bolte hai, dance floor pe laao,
Woh jahan bhi jayenge, wahan party shuru karo.
Aankhon mein sparkle, aur baaton mein masti,
Unke saath har din, ek dum hi fantastic.
Har din ek naya twist, har baat ek joke,
Unka style hai unique, jaise ek rockstar.
Secrets reveal karte hue, woh banaate hai scene,
Anurag ke saath time, hai like a Bollywood dream.
Toh jab bhi Anurag ki yaad aaye, hansi aayegi zaroor,
Woh mentor hai sabse cool, jo banate hai sabko khush aur
poora.
Chhoti si pony aur unke funny lines,
Anurag hai boss, aur unki style hai best in all times."

As the saying goes, "Haar ke jeetne waale ko baazigar kehte hain."

CHAPTER SEVEN

MENTOR'S LIGHT, MY JOURNEY

The dream that seemed just out of reach. Despite scoring only a band 6 on the IELTS repeatedly, I refused to lose hope. London was always in my sights, a beacon guiding my path, and I knew deep down that someday I would achieve my goal of going there for my master's. The journey was tough, filled with moments of doubt and fear, especially when I couldn't crack the IELTS. But I held onto the belief that persistence would eventually pay off. In the midst of this struggle, Anurag and I had our share of fights. It wasn't all smooth sailing—there were tears, arguments, and the pain of not being understood. But just as quickly as we fought, we would reunite, stronger than before. Our bond wasn't just built on care and guidance; it was also forged in the fires of conflict and resolution. Each fight taught us more about each other and solidified our shared goal. After one particularly intense argument, we decided that I should try the PTE exam. But the stress and chaos took a toll on me. I questioned whether I would ever achieve my London dream. The pressure was immense, and I was so scared that I barely focused on my preparation. I remember the night before the exam in Ahmedabad, studying in a state of panic, wondering if I'd ever break this cycle of near-misses.

Anurag stayed in touch the entire time, guiding me from afar as I took the exam alone. When I returned to G9, anxiety filled the air. We discussed what might come next, both of us focused on the goal of getting me to the UK. But fate had other plans. While I was waiting for my result, my best friend Khushboo received her visa to the UK. We had started this journey together, but now I was stuck, and she was preparing to fly. Despite the mixed emotions, I was genuinely happy for her. We celebrated her success with a glittering night at Ajit Bhawan, filled with songs, laughter, and a sense of gratefulness. It was one of those magical nights that, despite everything, made me feel hopeful.

Finally, the day came when I received my PTE result. The suspense was overwhelming. When I saw that I had cleared the exam, it was a moment of pure joy mixed with relief. We celebrated, but it was also a deeply emotional moment—tears of happiness and a sense of achievement after so much struggle. Although I missed the September intake, we immediately began preparing for January. The dream was alive again, and with Anurag's guidance, the path forward seemed clearer.

This journey was more than just about passing an exam; it was about perseverance, the power of mentorship, and the importance of never giving up, no matter how many times you stumble. This story isn't just about passing an exam or reaching a destination. It's about the journey, the people who walk it with you, and the lessons you learn along the way. Anurag taught me that setbacks are just setups for comebacks and that with the right mentor by your side, any dream is within reach.

Life Lessons and Cultural Commentary

Throughout my journey, one big lesson stood out: **resilience**. The dream of going to London felt like chasing a faraway star. Scoring Band 6 repeatedly on the IELTS was frustrating, but it taught me that sticking with it and not giving up is what really matters. Each time I stumbled, I learned that real success isn't about winning right away but about being strong enough to keep going despite the challenges.

My experiences with Anurag showed me that relationships, whether with friends or mentors, grow stronger through conflict. We had our share of fights, filled with tears and frustration, but these struggles deepened our connection. Each argument and resolution became a lesson in **empathy and understanding.** Anurag's constant support, even when things were tough, showed me that good guidance isn't just about giving answers but about standing by someone through hard times.

When we decided to switch from the IELTS to the PTE exam, it highlighted the need to be flexible. Sometimes, the traditional methods don't work, and it's important to explore new options. This shift reflects a broader trend in society where rigid systems are questioned, and more personalized approaches are becoming important.

Watching my best friend Khushboo get her UK visa while I was still waiting was a mix of emotions. It showed me how personal achievements can intersect with cultural expectations. In a society that often measures success through big milestones like studying abroad, seeing a friend succeed while facing delays yourself can be tough. Yet, it's important to celebrate others' successes while still pursuing your own goals, no matter the challenges.

Finally, when I got my PTE results, the joy and relief were huge. It wasn't just about passing the exam but about realizing that **success is a journey,** not just a destination. The path to achieving a dream is full of ups and downs, and the true value comes from the effort and growth along the way. My story proves that every setback is a chance for a comeback and that **embracing the journey** and the people who support you is what really matters.

As Winston Churchill once said, *"Success is not final, failure is not fatal:* It is the courage to continue that counts." This quote embodies the spirit of my journey. No matter how many times I stumbled, the courage to keep going kept me moving forward.

Another inspiring thought is from Nelson Mandela, who wisely noted, *"It always seems impossible until it's done."* This perfectly captures the essence of my struggle and eventual triumph. The dream of studying in London seemed far-fetched at times, but perseverance turned it into reality.

Lastly, I remind myself of a quote by Ralph Waldo Emerson: "What lies behind us and what lies before us are tiny matters compared to what lies within us." It was the inner strength, determination, and unwavering support from mentors like Anurag that truly made a difference. The journey was not just about reaching a destination but about discovering my own resilience and capabilities along the way.

Hey Diary,

Oh, what a whirlwind it's been! My life's been like a rollercoaster ride with no brakes, and I'm just hanging on tight, hoping it'll steer me toward something spectacular. Let me take you through this wild adventure I've been loving lately.

London has always been my North Star, my ultimate dream that seemed like it was just out of reach. Every time I tried to grasp it, my IELTS scores felt like a roadblock, saying, "Not today, champ." Scoring Band 6 time and again was like being caught in a never-ending loop of disappointment. But quitting? That was never on the cards. I held onto the belief that persistence is the key to success.

Now, let me tell you about Anurag. He's like a whirlwind of energy, always up to something unpredictable. Our relationship has had its fair share of fireworks—think Bollywood drama with fewer dance numbers and more heated debates. Each argument was like a plot twist, but they always ended with us coming back stronger, like a phoenix rising from the ashes. If our story were a movie, it'd be packed with passionate spats and heartfelt reconciliations, set to a soundtrack of us finding our way back to each other.

One of our biggest plot twists came when we decided to switch gears and try the PTE exam. It was a rollercoaster ride in itself. I remember the night before the exam in Ahmedabad, I was a bundle of nerves, cramming like there was no tomorrow and wondering if this was all worth it. The anxiety was palpable, and so was the fear that my London dream might be slipping through my fingers.

But Anurag didn't let me crash and burn. Even from afar, his words were like a safety net, catching me every time I started to wobble. Returning to G9 after the exam felt like coming back from a battlefield, only to face a new set of challenges. The atmosphere was charged with anticipation and stress. And just when I thought I was at my lowest, Khushboo, my best friend, got her UK visa. We started this journey together, and now she was flying off while I was still grounded. It was a cocktail of happiness for her and frustration for me.

Even though the emotional rollercoaster was a lot to handle, her victory was a reminder of why we keep fighting. We celebrated her success with a night at Ajit Bhawan, filled with music, laughter, and a whole lot of sparkle. It was like a scene straight out of a Bollywood movie—joyous, glittery, and just what I needed to keep my spirits high.

Then came the day of my PTE results. The suspense was like waiting for the climax of a thriller movie. When I finally saw that I'd passed, it was a cocktail of relief and triumph. The tears flowed, not just from joy but from the weight of everything we'd been through. Missing the September intake was a bump in the road, but the goal remained: January was our new target, and the dream was still on the horizon.

This journey has taught me more than just how to ace an exam. It's about resilience, mentorship, and not letting go of your dreams, even when the path seems like a maze. Anurag's guidance has been like a lighthouse in a storm, showing me that setbacks are just setups for comebacks. With his support and a relentless spirit, I know London is just a step away.

So, here's to this incredible journey—full of unexpected turns, heart-stopping moments, and the people who make it all worthwhile. Here's to keeping the dream alive and making it to the next chapter, where hopefully, London will finally be within reach.

Catch you later,

Anurag,

CHAPTER EIGHT

SYMBOLISM IN THE JOURNEY:

1. London as the North Star:

- *Detail:* London represents the ultimate destination, akin to the North Star guiding sailors through uncharted waters. It stands as a shining beacon, a distant but achievable dream that directs and inspires every action taken along the way.

- *Moral:* Just as the North Star provides direction to travellers, having a clear and meaningful goal gives purpose to one's efforts. Even when the path seems long and challenging, holding on to a guiding dream helps navigate through the journey.

2. The IELTS Exam as a Gatekeeper:

- *Detail:* The IELTS exam symbolizes the barrier or gatekeeper that stands between the protagonist and their dream. Each Band 6 score represents a test of endurance, revealing the difficulty of crossing this threshold to reach the desired destination.

- *Moral:* Gatekeepers in life often test our resolve. Each challenge faced is an opportunity to grow stronger and more determined. Persistence in overcoming these barriers is crucial for achieving success.

3. Anurag's Guidance as a Beacon of Light:

- *Detail:* Anurag's mentorship symbolizes a beacon of light in the midst of uncertainty. His advice and unwavering support serve as a constant source of guidance, helping the protagonist navigate through the trials and tribulations of their journey.

- *Moral:* True mentorship illuminates the path during dark times. A supportive guide helps clarify the direction and provides encouragement, making it easier to persevere through difficult moments.

4. The PTE Exam as a New Pathway:

- *Detail:* Opting for the PTE exam after struggling with IELTS represents a new path or alternative route to reach the dream. It signifies the need to adapt and find new solutions when traditional methods do not yield results.

- *Moral:* Flexibility and innovation are key to overcoming obstacles. When the usual methods fail, exploring new approaches can open doors to success and help achieve goals in unexpected ways.

5. Khushboo's Visa as a Mirror of Success:

- *Detail:* Khushboo's success in obtaining her UK visa, while the protagonist is still waiting, mirrors societal expectations and the personal impact of seeing peers achieve milestones. It reflects the intersection of personal aspirations with external measures of success.

- *Moral:* Celebrating others' achievements while facing personal setbacks can be challenging but important. It reminds us to appreciate others' successes and stay motivated to pursue our own goals despite delays.

6. The Night at Ajit Bhawan as a Spark of Hope:

- *Detail:* The celebratory night at Ajit Bhawan symbolizes a moment of joy and renewed optimism. Amidst the struggle, this event provides a much-needed respite and rekindles hope, serving as a reminder that joy can be found even in tough times.

- *Moral:* Finding moments of celebration and joy during challenging times is crucial for maintaining motivation and positivity. These moments can reignite hope and provide the strength to continue pursuing one's goals.

7. The PTE Results as a Turning Point:

- *Detail:* Receiving the PTE results marks a significant turning point in the journey. It represents the culmination of effort and perseverance, turning the long-anticipated dream into a reality and signifying a major breakthrough.

- *Moral:* Key milestones in our journey often represent a turning point. The culmination of hard work and persistence leads to moments of achievement that validate the effort and reinforce the belief in achieving one's dreams.

8. The Journey as a Testament to Resilience:

- *Detail:* The entire journey symbolizes resilience and perseverance. The ups and downs, the repeated attempts, and the eventual success all reflect the protagonist's strength and determination in the face of continuous challenges.

- *Moral:* Life's journey is a testament to our resilience. True success is not just about the result but also about the perseverance and strength demonstrated throughout the process.

9. The Path Forward as a New Chapter:

- *Detail:* Preparing for the January intake symbolizes the start of a new chapter after missing the September intake. It signifies a fresh start and the continued pursuit of the dream, embodying the idea of moving forward despite setbacks.

- *Moral:* Every setback is an opportunity for a new beginning. Embracing new chapters with renewed determination keeps the journey alive and opens new possibilities for achieving goals.

CHAPTER NINE

THE RISHIKESH REVERIE WITH SUICIDE SQUAD

"Sapno ki udan hai, manzilon ka ehsaas hai,
Rishte jo junoon se bane, unmein hi toh
vishwas hai."

"

Our dream begins with a shared vision, a magical illusion we've both cherished—a trip to Rishikesh, with the squad the land of spirituality, serenity, and sacredness. This isn't just any trip; it's a journey where our dreams merge, creating an experience that feels so real, that it's as if the gods themselves blessed it.

"ये सफर भी अजीब था, ख़्वाबों में रचा-बसा,
पलकों पे सजा, फिर दिल में बसा।"
We always dreamed of that flight from Jodhpur to
Dehradun,
Rishikesh in our hearts, our souls attuned.

Pink top, white bottoms, hair with a gleam,
Boarding that flight, living our dream.
Delhi's lounge, with food so divine,
Veggies and rice, a moment to unwind.
On to Dehradun, where the hills stood tall,
Cool breezes whispered, "Welcome, y'all."
Finally, Rishikesh, where the sunsets glow,
Dehradun to Rishikesh, our excitement flowed.
Checked into a hotel, cozy and warm,
Dinner by the Ganga, a magical charm.
Under the tree, with the lamp's soft light,
We talked and laughed, through the cold, crisp night.
Next morning on bikes, we roamed the hills,
With Maggie in hand, we chased our thrills.
Evening brought the Ganga Aarti's grace,
A memory etched, in time and space.
But just like every tale, chaos found its way,
In our dream trip, it came to play.
Anurag, the anchor, firm and secure,
Tried to keep me grounded, steady and pure.
I was the wild one, with a heart so free,
And often, we'd clash, as you might see.
"Focus on studies, on dreams that gleam,
Don't lose your way, in life's wild stream."
But our bond was strong, even with the fights,
We found our way back, under the starry nights.
"सपनो की वो दुनिया, हकीकत से प्यारी,
हर पल में बसी, एक नयी खुमारी।
रशिकिश की वो रातें, यादो में सजी,"
This Rishikesh tale, a journey so fine,
In our hearts forever, a memory divine.
No matter the chaos, or the storms that blow,
Our bond, like the Ganga, continues to flow.
"

Like any other relationship, ours was a mix of love and chaos. There were times when we fought, and while we usually reunited quickly, this time was different. Imagine a month of silence between us—no communication, no contact. It was unthinkable, considering how much we had supported each other. This twist in our story was unexpected and taught us a lot about the strength of our bond. In the end, the Rishikesh trip, though just an illusion, reflected our reality. It was a journey of highs and lows, dreams and reality, love and conflict. But most importantly, it was a reminder that no matter the challenges, our connection was strong enough to overcome them and that our dreams—whether real or imagined—always had the potential to come true. After everything we'd shared, suddenly, formality crept in like an unwanted guest. Our bond, once so close and effortless, began to feel restrained. It was as if we had drifted into different worlds, only acknowledging each other with polite exchanges. I was focused on my visa, hoping to finally set foot in the UK by January. We applied with high hopes, but, as with every chapter of our story, drama was never far behind. This time, the twist came when my visa was put on hold. Everyone else from my batch had already flown to their destinations, but I was stuck, waiting in limbo. It was a frustrating time, filled with doubts and fears. But I held onto hope, knowing that setbacks are just stepping stones in the journey to success. During this period, our bond, which had taken a hit, slowly began to mend. We reconnected at a wedding, and the excitement of meeting him again brought back all those feelings that had been buried under the weight of formality. It was as if time had rewound, and we were back where we started, with the same warmth and understanding.

This chapter is a reminder that no matter how tough things get, patience and perseverance can overcome any obstacle. The visa may have been delayed, but the bond we shared found its way back, stronger and more resilient than before.

Our Rishikesh trip was more than just a journey—it was a dream stitched into reality, an adventure where each moment was a riddle, and every experience felt as if touched by divine hands. This chapter unfolds through riddles, flashbacks, and surreal moments, exploring the deeper layers of our bond and the trials we faced.

Riddle of the Bond:

"In a land where serenity meets the river's flow,
Where dreams take shape and true colors show,
What keeps two hearts, though tested and strained,
Bound together, despite being pained?"

Answer: The Journey and Its Challenges

Our trip to Rishikesh, with its moments of joy and conflict, became a metaphor for our relationship. It was a journey marked by dreams and reality, where every twist and turn revealed new facets of our bond.

Flashback to the Beginning:

In the days leading up to our Rishikesh adventure, life was a dance of separation and individuality. I was immersed in my world, where everything was ordered and predictable. Then entered Anurag—like a burst of colour in a monochrome canvas. Meeting him for the first time was akin to witnessing a meteor shower; his presence was overwhelming, and his energy was a sharp contrast to my own quiet demeanour.

Our initial interactions felt like the collision of two cosmic bodies. Anurag's enthusiasm and spontaneity were like a blazing comet, while I was more like a distant, reserved star. The sparks from our clash were undeniable—fiery debates and intense discussions that seemed to shake the very foundation of our newly formed relationship.

Despite this friction, an undercurrent of mutual respect ran through our exchanges. Beneath the surface of our disagreements, there was a shared vision—a common goal that bridged our contrasting personalities. Our early conversations, often laced with riddles and cryptic phrases, were a testament to this bond. Anurag had a unique way of challenging me, weaving his words into puzzles that demanded not just answers but deeper understanding. He would often speak in enigmatic terms, like a philosopher with secrets waiting to be unravelled. For instance, he might say, "In the labyrinth of life, only those who seek the hidden pathways find their way." These riddles weren't just playful banter; they were invitations to look beyond the surface, to engage in a deeper exploration of our thoughts and aspirations. This cryptic dialogue wasn't merely a test of wit but a way for Anurag to encourage me to expand my thinking and embrace uncertainty. Each riddle was a mirror reflecting our evolving relationship, filled with complexities and depth. Our exchanges, though sometimes contentious, were also moments of discovery—learning about each other's perspectives, values, and dreams.

Through these interactions, I began to appreciate the layers of Anurag's character. What initially seemed like a clash of worlds evolved into a dynamic partnership, where our contrasting traits complemented rather than clashed. The riddles became symbols of our journey, representing the ongoing process of unraveling each other's complexities and finding common ground amid our differences.

Thus, our story began with a blend of fiery clashes and cryptic challenges, setting the stage for a relationship that would grow through both conflict and collaboration. It was in these moments of tension and mystery that the foundation for our future was laid, characterized by a unique mix of understanding, respect, and shared dreams.

Surreal Moment:

"In dreams, we drift to realms afar,
Where the Ganga flows beneath a silver star.
What is this place where reality bends,
Where dreams and memories seamlessly blend?"

Answer: The Land of Dreams and Reflections
A Riddle of the Heart:

""Amidst the chaos, where silence reigns,
What stirs the heart, despite the strains?
When formality creeps and warmth seems lost,
What revives the bond, no matter the cost?""

Answer: Reconnection and Shared Moments

When our communication faltered, and formality crept in like a shadow, it was the shared moments—like the wedding—that reignited our connection. The excitement of seeing Anurag again was like a jolt of electricity, restoring the warmth that had been missing. The wedding was more than just an event; it was a turning point, reminding us of the deep bond we shared.

The Resilient Connection:

""A bridge built on dreams, though storms may roar,
Stands firm and unyielding, forevermore.
What is this bridge, that time cannot sever,
A bond so resilient, it holds on forever?""

Answer: The Strong Connection We Share

Our relationship, like a bridge built on dreams and shared experiences, proved resilient through all trials. The delays and formality were just storms that tested the strength of our bond. The reunion at the wedding was a testament to the fact that no matter how turbulent the journey, our connection remained strong.

Flashback: The Visa Wait

The wait for my visa was a particularly trying period. Every day felt like an eternity as I watched others move ahead while I remained in limbo. The frustration was palpable, and the dream of reaching the UK seemed increasingly distant. Yet, through this period of waiting, I learned valuable lessons about patience and perseverance. Each setback was a stepping stone, and every moment of doubt was a chance to reinforce my resolve.

Surreal Reflection:

""In the land where time stands still,
Where hope and despair are threads to distill,
What guides us through the darkest hour,
And turns trials into a blooming flower?""

Answer: Hope and Determination

In the surreal moments of waiting, hope and determination were my guiding stars. They turned the trials into opportunities for growth and kept my spirit alive. The experience taught me that every challenge, no matter how daunting, could be transformed into a moment of strength and learning.

Ambiguous Endings:

The journey's end is as elusive as the dream itself. Did we truly reach Rishikesh, or was it merely a vision that played out in our minds? The line between reality and illusion often blurs, leaving us to question the nature of our experiences. As we moved through the days, was it the anticipation or the actual journey that shaped our memories?

When formality slipped in, did we lose a piece of our connection, or was it merely a new phase in our evolving bond? Did the wedding reunion rekindle our warmth, or did it mask a deeper shift in our relationship? The answers remain open, inviting you to ponder the nuances of our journey and the ongoing evolution of our connection.

Reflective Epilogue:

Our story, rich with riddles and reflections, is a testament to the enduring power of resilience and connection. From the vibrant yet chaotic trip to Rishikesh to the trials of visa delays, every twist and turn has sculpted our bond into something profoundly resilient.

In the end, it's not just about reaching a destination but about the journey itself—the moments of chaos and clarity, of dreams woven with reality. Our connection, tested through conflict and formality, proved to be a bridge that withstood the storms of time and distance.

As we look back on our adventure, we find that the true essence of our story lies in the lessons learned and the bond that emerged stronger through every trial. The journey may have been filled with uncertainties and ambiguous endings, but it has also been a journey of growth, discovery, and unbreakable connection.

So here's to the dream that led us through the highs and lows, to the moments that defined us, and to the bond that remains unyielding, no matter where our paths may lead. The journey continues, and with each new chapter, we find new ways to embrace the dreams and challenges that lie ahead.

Now, with renewed enthusiasm, we look forward to the next chapter, knowing that every setback is just a setup for a greater comeback.

CHAPTER TEN

"The Clash of Cosmos: Love, Rules, and Reconciliation"

Prologue: The Cosmic Clash

In the grand theatre of our lives, where the vast expanse of the cosmos mirrors our universe, the saga of Anurag and I begins. Picture a celestial stage, where stars burn with intense energy and planets move with deliberate precision. Here, our lives are not merely intertwined but are a dramatic dance of cosmic proportions. Anurag, with his fiery, unyielding presence, was like a blazing supernova—brilliant, unpredictable, and immensely powerful. His temper was a storm that could light up the dark void of our interactions with its intensity. On the other hand, I was a comet, streaking through the universe with a mix of wild abandon and controlled trajectory.

Our relationship was akin to two celestial bodies in a gravitational tug-of-war. Anurag's guidance was relentless and exacting, setting rigid boundaries that felt like the gravitational pull of a black hole, drawing everything toward him, demanding compliance. I, with my rebellious streak and unrestrained spirit, was often caught in the crossfire of this cosmic struggle. My orbit around his rules was erratic, and the push and pull between us created a celestial phenomenon of its own—a display of passion and discipline colliding in an intricate dance of love and conflict.

As we navigated this cosmic ballet, each argument and reconciliation was like a meteor shower—a spectacular, often messy, explosion of emotions that left trails of stardust in its wake. The drama of our interactions was as unpredictable as the movements of the stars, and every clash was a testament to the intense gravitational forces at play. Despite the chaos, there was a certain beauty to our conflict, like watching the celestial dance of a galaxy in turmoil.

This prologue sets the stage for a story where the cosmic metaphor not only reflects the scale of our struggles but also hints at the grandeur of our reconciliation. It's a reminder that in the universe of our relationship, every clash, every resolution, contributes to the ever-evolving constellation of our shared journey.

Dream Sequence: The Battle of the Stars

In the tranquil hush of night's embrace, I slipped into a cosmic space, where the universe transformed before my eyes, into a grand chessboard under starlit skies. On this celestial field, Anurag and I took our places, each of us with our cosmic faces. I stood on one side, he on the other, and every piece we moved was like no other.

The sky above, a canvas of shimmering lights, unveiled constellations in whispered heights. Our arguments became knights, fierce and bold, charging forth, their stories told. Pawns represented the fears we kept, while rooks embodied the pride we'd swept. Bishops, our dreams, traced diagonal paths, leading us through life's inevitable wraths.

The queen of hope sparkled in the dark, while kings of doubt left their mark. We moved our pieces with strategic grace, as stars above set the pace. Each shift and turn on this cosmic board mirrored our clashes, our hearts implored.

The celestial game was a dance of emotion, a swirling blend of passion and devotion. Each piece on the board told a tale, a symbol of our love that could never fail. With every move, the constellations sang a symphony of our journey and the change it brings.

As the game neared its twilight phase, our pieces aligned in a celestial blaze. The cosmic struggle found its end, and we saw our hearts on a path to mend. The stars above, with their gentle light, mirrored our reconciliation in the still of the night.

In this dreamscape of cosmic play, we found our fears and hopes in a new way. The grand chessboard of the stars showed us the intricate dance of our hearts, a reflection of battles fought and peace sought, under the endless sky where dreams are caught.

The Rules of Engagement

Anurag had a strict set of rules, which I learned about quickly and clearly. His way of leading was more about asserting control than offering guidance. His demands felt less like helpful advice and more like a comprehensive overhaul of my life. He insisted that I sever all connections with everyone outside of our immediate circle. This meant cutting off friends and, most critically, my boyfriend. To him, my social world was a mere extension of his authority, and he sought to limit it as he saw fit.

It wasn't just about telling me who I could or couldn't interact with. Anurag took it a step further by actively monitoring my social media accounts. His habit of checking my profiles and scrutinizing every post or message added a layer of surveillance to his control. Whenever we had disagreements or arguments, his response was to block me from all social media platforms. This wasn't just about removing access—it was a dramatic declaration of power, a visible reminder of who was in charge.

These blocks felt like more than mere interruptions; they were deliberate actions intended to assert his dominance. Each time he did it, it was as if he was drawing a boundary around me, one that he controlled. My online presence became a restricted zone, a place where Anurag's authority reigned supreme.

Every interaction, every message, and every post was scrutinized under his watchful eye. My social media accounts, once a space for personal expression and connection, became a controlled environment, managed and monitored by Anurag. His rules transformed my freedom into a series of constraints, leaving me with little autonomy in the digital world.

Living under his stringent regulations, my world was consistently reshaped to fit his demands. My social interactions were reduced to a delicate dance around his rules. Each block, each demand, each check felt like a tug-of-war over control. This constant intervention turned my social life into a battleground, where my connections and freedoms were continually tested by his need for dominance.

In this atmosphere of control, every decision felt weighed down by the threat of restriction. Anurag's rules didn't just limit my interactions; they reshaped my reality, making every aspect of my social life subject to his approval and control.

In his eyes, the world outside was a potential threat to my academic success, and his methods were as strict as they were unconventional.

"Block the world, focus on the dream," he'd say, his words as forceful as the winds of a storm.

Our fights were not just personal spats; they were epic confrontations, full of emotional drama and intense exchanges. Anurag had this habit of checking my phone with a frequency that could only be described as obsessive. Whenever we disagreed, he'd retaliate by blocking me from Snapchat—each block a symbolic shutout, a way to reassert control.

The irony of it all was that while Anurag was pushing me to excel, I found myself drawn back into a relationship with my boyfriend. This rebellion was a secret I was terrified to share. Anurag, being the best mentor, had a reputation for both fierce guidance and a stern demeanour. I feared his reaction, knowing how much he prioritized my studies. To confess that I had resumed contact with my boyfriend felt like admitting to a major transgression.

And then, it happened—a confrontation of such magnitude that it felt like a tempest had descended upon us. Our biggest fight erupted in early December, and the drama was so intense that it felt as if the entire universe had taken sides. The irony was not lost on me: on December 4th, the day of our explosive argument, I had to face the fact that Anurag's birthday was just two days away, on December 6th. I couldn't bring myself to wish him. The person who had been my mentor, my guide, was now estranged from me, and the chasm felt insurmountable.

In the following month, the silence was deafening. I stayed away from G9, avoiding the very place that had once been a beacon of hope and guidance. It was as though the universe had hit a pause on our relationship. But, as always, fate had a way of weaving its threads back together. By January, the storm had passed. The fight that had once seemed monumental now felt like a distant echo. We slowly reconnected, albeit with a formality that masked the deep-seated emotions we both felt.

This period of estrangement, while painful, taught us an invaluable lesson. It was a testament to the resilience of our bond, a bond that could withstand even the most intense conflicts. As the New Year rolled in, our reconciliation was bittersweet. We didn't celebrate the new year together, nor did we acknowledge each other's presence in the traditional sense. Yet, as the days passed, the cracks in our relationship began to mend, revealing the strength and depth that had always been there.

The tumultuous nature of our interactions—the fights, the silences, and the eventual reunion—was a reflection of the complexities of human connections. Our story wasn't just about the highs and lows; it was about the unseen forces at play, the cosmic dance of relationships, and the recognition that sometimes, even the most intense battles can lead to a renewed understanding and closeness.

The final chapter of my journey with Anurag isn't just about the conflicts we had; it's about the strength of our relationship. Every argument, every period of silence, and every time we made up again revealed how strong our bond was. Our fights felt huge, like epic battles, because we both cared so much. Anurag's strict guidance and my rebellious nature often clashed, but this tension showed how deeply connected we were. The drama between us was a sign of how much we meant to each other, even when we disagreed.

Even in the heat of our arguments, I always knew that we would find our way back to each other. The times we didn't speak weren't just moments of silence; they were opportunities for both of us to reflect and grow. These quiet moments allowed us to heal and come back stronger. As we worked through the challenges in our relationship, it became clear that our bond wasn't about avoiding conflict, but about our ability to overcome it together. The cracks in our relationship during tough times weren't signs of weakness; they showed the depth and strength that had always been there. Over time, we learned to repair these cracks, not by ignoring them, but by addressing them and becoming even closer.

Our journey proved that even the toughest battles can lead to a stronger bond if faced with honesty and a willingness to make things right. In the end, our story wasn't just about the conflicts we faced, but about our commitment to always finding our way back to each other, no matter what.

In the end, this chapter is not just a recounting of conflict but a celebration of the resilience and depth of our bond. It was a reminder that even in the face of the most dramatic disagreements, the heart of our relationship remained steadfast, always finding its way back to each other.

CHAPTER ELEVEN

THE GRAND FINALE—A BREAKUP, A VISA, A DREAM, AND THE UNBREAKABLE BOND

Finally, after all the ups and downs, the fights, the reconciliations, and the endless drama, we found ourselves back to where it all began—back to the basics, back to G9. It was as if life had come full circle. But this time, there was a different vibe, a sense of calm and normalcy that we hadn't felt in a while. Every visit to G9 became a lesson in life, a moment to reconnect and motivate each other.

Every time we fought, every time we disagreed, it only made our bond stronger. G9 was our haven, our sanctuary where nothing else mattered but the connection we shared. It was our Bollywood movie, complete with love, fights, and the thrill of the unknown.

In June, the big plan was set in motion. We decided to apply for the September visa, and as always, nothing was ever simple with me. Everything took time, and the suspense kept us on the edge. The wait was intense, every day felt like a cliffhanger, just like a Bollywood movie where the hero's fate hangs in the balance. "Will she get the visa, or will she be left behind once again?" The tension was real, but so was the determination. With Anurag by my side, guiding me, pushing me, and sometimes pulling me back when I needed it, I knew deep down that this time, things would be different.

July arrived with its monsoon showers, and with it came the long-awaited news—**"The Visa Approved!"**

It was like the final scene in a blockbuster, where everything falls into place, and the hero finally achieves what they've been striving for. The excitement was palpable, the joy uncontainable. We celebrated like never before—laughing, crying, eating, and revisiting all the memories that brought us to this point. We relived the days spent at G9, the endless conversations, the lessons learned, and the food shared. Every bite of our favourite dishes was a taste of nostalgia, every laughs a reminder of how far we'd come. It was a Bollywood masala movie in every sense—full of drama, emotion, and a finale that left everyone cheering. And now, as I prepare to fly to the UK, it feels like the beginning of a new chapter, not just in my life, but in our story. The love, the fights, the endless lessons—everything has led to this moment. It's a blockbuster ending, but it's also the start of something even bigger. The credits may roll, but the story continues, just like in every great movie. So here's to the journey, the lessons, and the memories. Here's to the bond that no fight can break and no distance can weaken. Here's to the Bollywood blockbuster that is our life, and the exciting sequel that's about to unfold.

After everything we went through—the ups and downs, the arguments and make-ups, the endless twists and turns—we found ourselves right back where it all started: G9. But this time, it felt different. There was a calmness, a sense of peace like the storm had finally passed. G9 wasn't just an office anymore; it had become our haven, a place where we could reconnect and draw strength from each other.

Every disagreement we had, and every challenge we faced, didn't weaken our bond; it made it stronger. G9 was where we could leave all the drama behind and focus on what really mattered—our connection. It was our personal Bollywood film, filled with love, conflict, and the thrill of uncertainty. The more we fought, the more we realized how much we meant to each other, and how much we needed G9 as our anchor.

Then came June, and with it, the big decision to apply for the September visa. Of course, in true dramatic fashion, nothing was straightforward. Everything seemed to take longer than expected, and the suspense kept us on edge. It was like living in a Bollywood movie where you're constantly wondering if the hero will make it to the end. Every day was a cliffhanger—"Will the visa come through, or will everything fall apart again?" The tension was high, but so was our determination. With Anurag by my side, guiding me, challenging me, and pulling me back when I was about to lose focus, I felt a deep sense of certainty that this time, things would be different.

And then July came, bringing with it the monsoon rains and the news we had been waiting for: "Visa Approved!" It was like the final, triumphant scene in a blockbuster movie, where everything finally falls into place. The joy was overwhelming, the relief indescribable. We celebrated as if it were the biggest victory of our lives—laughing, crying, and reminiscing about all the moments that had led us to this point.

We spent those days at G9, reliving the memories, talking about the lessons learned, and enjoying the food we loved. Every bite was filled with nostalgia, every laugh a reminder of the journey we had shared. It was like a Bollywood masala movie—full of drama, emotions, and a perfect ending that left us all feeling elated.

Now, as I prepare to fly to the UK, it feels like the closing of one chapter and the beginning of another. Our story isn't ending; it's just evolving. The love, the fights, the lessons we've learned—everything has brought us to this moment. It's the grand finale of one part of our journey, but also the exciting start of something even bigger. The credits might be rolling on this chapter, but our story is far from over. There's a sequel waiting to unfold, filled with new adventures, challenges, and memories yet to be made.

So here's to the journey we've had, the lessons we've learned, and the bond that has only grown stronger through it all. Here's to the Bollywood blockbuster that has been our life, and the new chapter that's just beginning.

> ""*Aankhon mein sapne liye, G9 se hum chale,*
> *Zindagi ke raaste par, khwab saath le chale.*"
>
> *(With dreams in our eyes, we set out from G9,*
> *On the path of life, taking our dreams along.)*
> "*Chand sa roshan chehra, jugnu si yeh raahein,*
> *Mile the hum jahaan, yaadon ki hai baatein.*"
>
> *(Your face shines like the moon, the paths glow like fireflies,*
> *Where we met, those are tales of memories.)*
> "*Tujhse naraz nahin zindagi, hairan hoon main,*
> *G9 ka rishta, beparwah hoon main.*"
> *(I'm not angry at life, just amazed,*
> *Our G9 bond, carefree, I embrace.)*
> "*Kabhi kabhi Aditi zindagi mein yunhi,*
> *Koi apna lagta hai.*"
> *(Sometimes in life, Aditi, it just feels,*
> *Like someone becomes your own.)*
> "*Ae zindagi gale laga le, humne bhi tere har ik gham*
> *ko gale se lagaya hai,*"
>
> *(O life, embrace me, as I've embraced every sorrow you've*
> *shown me.)*
> "*Tera mujhse hai pehle ka naata koi,*
> *Yuhi nahin dil lubhata koi.*"

(There's an ancient bond between you and me,
It's not for nothing that my heart is drawn to thee.)
"Humne dekhi hai in aankhon ki mehekti khushboo,
Haath se chooke ise rishton ka ilzaam na do."
(I've seen the fragrance in your eyes,
Don't blame this touch on any ties.)
"Kabhi alvida na kehna, hum milenge phir se,
Visa aaya hai, sapna ab hai raaste mein."

(Never say goodbye, for we'll meet again,
The visa has come, and now the dream is on its way.)
"Tujhme rab dikhta hai, yaara main kya karoon,
G9 ka har pal, ab yaadon mein hai mehroom."
(I see God in you, my friend, what can I do?
Every moment of G9, now echoes in memory too.)
"Yeh honsla kaise jhuke, yeh arzoo kaise ruke,
G9 se udi yeh chidiya, ab UK mein apne sukh le."

(How can this courage falter? How can this desire stop?
From G9, this bird has flown, and now it rests in the UK's
comfort.)
"Zindagi ek safar hai suhana, yahan kal kya ho kisne
jaana,
Jee lo yeh pal, UK mein naya hai thikana."

(Life is a beautiful journey, who knows what tomorrow
holds,
Live this moment, a new home awaits in the UK, bold.)
"Pyar humein kis mod pe le aaya,
G9 ke yaadon se jud gaya hai saaya."

(Love has brought us to a new turn,
But the shadow of G9 memories will always yearn.)"

RIDDLE & PUZZLE

1.

I'm a place where dreams took flight, painted in Jodhpur's iconic blue light. Where lessons were learned, and bonds grew tight. What am I?

2.

He guided with care, sometimes with a stern glare. Told you to block, focus, and beware. Who is he?

3.

In a place where drama unfolds, with lessons, love, and stories untold. The journey begins with a visa to hold. What am I?

4.

You fought, you reconciled, and the bond stayed strong. Where did you find peace all along?

5.

This day brought tension and a fight, but two days later should have been bright. What was the occasion that was missed?

6.

He checked your phone, made you block and stray, but it was all to keep distractions at bay. Who was this guiding force, day by day?

7.

It felt like a movie with love, fights, and glee. But this moment of victory was like the final key. What event am I?

8.

You reunited after a storm of words, but it wasn't New Year's that mended the cords. What was the time that began your return to normalcy?

Puzzle: "The Journey of Anurag and Akshi"

Clues:

1. *Where it All Began: A place painted in Jodhpur's iconic blue, where a mentor met his match, and dreams took their first flight.* **(What is this place?)**
2. *A Guiding Star: He was more than just a mentor, guiding with wisdom and care, sometimes strict, but always with the best intentions at heart.* **(Who is he?)**
3. *The Secret Connection: Though known for his sternness, his guidance helped someone special, leading to an unexpected bond and countless memories shared.* **(Who is this bond with?)**

4. *A Turning Point: After an emotional journey of ups and downs, this event marked a significant moment of reconnection and renewal between them.* **(What event?)**

5. *Shared Lessons: In their journey, they learned and grew, with one always ready to guide and the other eager to learn. But it was also about something more, something deeper.* **(What did they learn about?)**

6. *A Special Place: This place, where emotions ran high, became a sanctuary, filled with memories, laughter, and the spirit of camaraderie.* **(What is this place?)**

7. *The Unspoken Bond: Despite the fights and misunderstandings, their connection endured, stronger after each conflict, deeper after each reconciliation.* **(What is the nature of this bond?)**

8. *The Final Step: This moment marked the completion of a journey, a milestone that was both an ending and a beginning.* **(What was this moment?)**

From Dreams To Triumph: A Journey Of Love, Struggle, And Victory

"

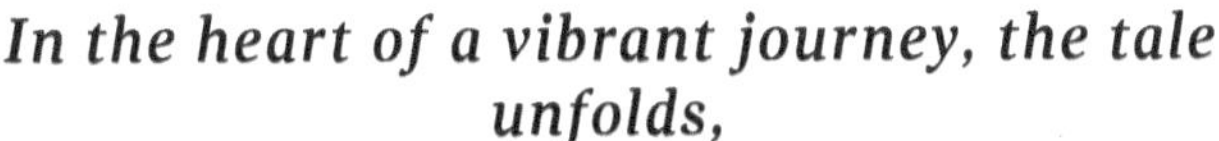

*In the heart of a vibrant journey, the tale
unfolds,*

*From Jodhpur's lanes to the UK's cold,
A story of dreams, love, and flight,
With twists and turns that light up the
night.*

*Chapter one set the scene, where dreams
took flight,
We faced the first hurdles with courage
and might.
From emotional bonds to formal ties,
We navigated the chaos with hopeful eyes.*

*In chapter two, a visa saga we pursued,
The anticipation, the struggle, the endless
wait, we knew.
Yet, through every trial and every test,
We held onto hope, giving it our best.*

*The vibrant scene,
With Bollywood beats and a trip that felt*

like a dream.
From partying to dancing through the
night,
The rhythm of our hearts was our guiding
light.

Chapter four brought a twist of fate,
With IELTS scores and a challenge to
navigate.
But through the stress and the high stakes,
We stood together, and our bond never
broke.

In chapter five, the fight and chaos are
unveiled,
But love and mentorship never failed.
Through sleepless nights and battles
fought,
The journey of dreams was always sought.

As the months went by, formalities grew,
With visa holds and dreams in view.
Yet, with every setback and every fall,
Our story remained, standing tall.

Finally, as we reached the grand finale,
With visa success and dreams so pally,
Our journey turned into a Bollywood song,
With love, fights, and memories lifelong.

And so we end with a grand, joyful cheer,
A tale of dreams, love, and every tear.
From Jodhpur to Rishikesh's embrace,
To the UK's horizon, we set our pace.

In every chapter, a lesson to find,
Through every struggle, a story
intertwined.
May our tale inspire and light up the dark,
Dreams, love, and hope are where we
embark.

Summary

In the heart of this novel lies a journey that mirrors life itself—full of dreams, challenges, friendships, and the unyielding spirit of perseverance.

The story begins with a young protagonist, full of ambition but also grappling with the uncertainty that comes with venturing into the unknown. From the moment they step into G9 Abroad Education, a world of possibilities opens up, one that promises not just academic success, but a deeper understanding of life. The protagonist's journey is anything but smooth. Balancing the pressures of office life with the demands of rigorous study, they face obstacles that would make even the strongest question their path. Yet, it is through these very challenges that they discover their resilience.

Every setback becomes a stepping stone, every doubt a call to action.

Along the way, the protagonist encounters a mentor in Anurag, who is more than just a guide; he is a beacon of hope and a reminder that true mentors do more than teach—they inspire. Their bond is one of mutual respect, filled with moments of joy, tension, and deep reflection. Through their interactions, the protagonist learns that life's greatest lessons often come not from books, but from the people we meet and the experiences we share.

The novel is rich with moments of introspection, but it is also alive with the vibrancy of youth—there are friendships formed, late-night study sessions, and moments of pure, unfiltered fun. The protagonist's journey is a testament to the power of determination and the importance of staying true to one's dreams, no matter the odds.

In the end, the story isn't just about getting a visa or achieving a goal; it's about the transformation that occurs along the way.

The protagonist emerges not just as someone who has succeeded in their academic pursuits, but as someone who has grown, who has learned to embrace the highs and lows of life, and who understands that the journey is just as important as the destination.

This novel serves as a powerful reminder that life is a beautiful blend of struggles and triumphs. It teaches us that while the road may be rocky, the strength to keep going lies within us. And most importantly, it reminds us that with the right mindset, the right people by our side, and the right amount of faith, anything is possible.

For anyone standing on the brink of a new journey, uncertain of what lies ahead, this story offers a message of hope: that no dream is too big, no challenge too great, and that with perseverance and passion, you can turn your aspirations into reality.

The novel leaves us with this final thought: *"Zindagi ek safar hai suhana."* Cherish every moment, face every challenge head-on, and never stop believing in the power of your dreams.